UNITED STATES OF AMERICA

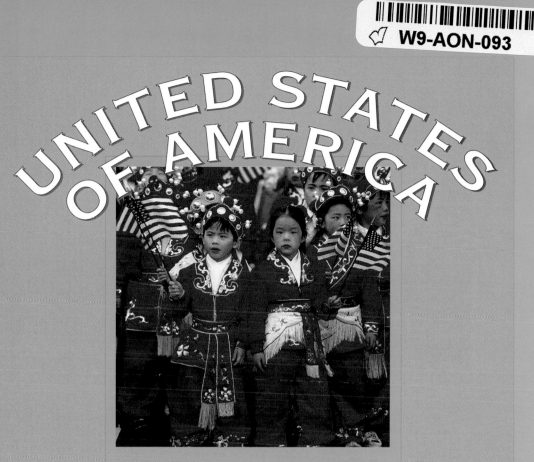

A TRUE BOOK

by

**Christine Petersen and
David Petersen**

Children's Press®

A Division of Scholastic Inc.

New York Toronto London Auckland Sydney
Mexico City New Delhi Hong Kong
Danbury, Connecticut

Mount Rushmore in South Dakota

Reading Consultant
Nanci R. Vargus, Ed.D.
*Primary Multiage Teacher
Decatur Township Schools,
Indianapolis, IN*

The photograph on the cover shows the Rocky Mountains. The photograph on the title page shows children at a Chinese New Year celebration in Los Angeles, California.

Library of Congress Cataloging-in-Publication Data

Petersen, Christine and David Petersen
   United States of America / by Christine Petersen and David Petersen.
      p. cm. — (A true book)
   Includes bibliographical references and index.
   ISBN 0-516-22259-7 (lib. bdg.) 0-516-27362-0 (pbk.)
    1. United States—Juvenile literature. [1. United States.]
 I. Petersen, Christine. II. Title. III. Series.
   E156.P452001
   973—dc21   00-047563

Contents

Pacific coastline
in Oregon

From Sea to Shining Sea

Stretching from the Pacific Ocean to the Atlantic Ocean, the United States of America is the fourth-largest country in the world. It includes a huge variety of landscapes. Blue-green mountains, flowering deserts, pancake plains, sandy beaches, rocky coasts, dense forests—these combine with vibrant cities to create a place that is home to 275 million people.

The United States has many great cities, including San Francisco (left) and New York (above).

Mount McKinley in Alaska (below) and Lumahai Beach in Kauai, Hawaii (right)

The United States can be divided into three regions: the forty-eight connected states, Alaska, and Hawaii. The forty-eight states lie between

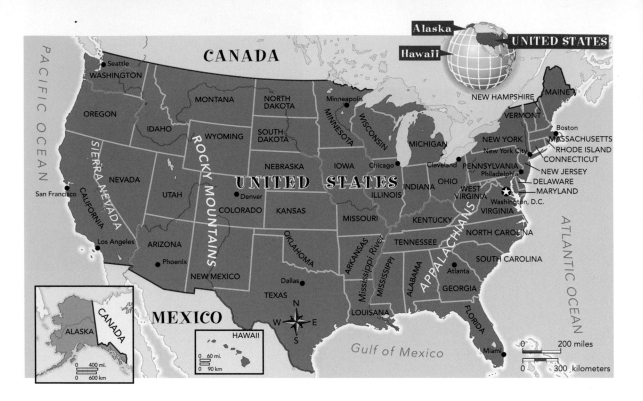

Canada to the north and Mexico to the south. Alaska is the northern tip of North America, north and west of Canada. Hawaii is a group of islands about 2,400 mi. (3,862 km) west of California in the Pacific Ocean.

The Appalachians, America's oldest mountains, run along the eastern edge of the United States. After millions of years of erosion, they are greatly worn, low, and rounded.

Out west, the much younger Rocky Mountains pierce the clouds with their jagged peaks. The Rockies are the highest and longest mountain range in North America. They begin in Alaska, stretch south through Canada and the United States, and end in Mexico. The spectacular Sierra

The Appalachian Mountains in Virginia (left) and the Rocky Mountains in Colorado (above)

Nevada runs along the western edge of the forty-eight states.

In between these three great mountain ranges is a vast patchwork of forests, deserts, and plains. Hundreds of lakes and rivers provide water and

A forest in Washington (left) and Death Valley in California (right)

power for the people and their industries.

Very little rain falls in the hot, rocky deserts lying south and west of the Rockies. Death Valley, in California's Mojave Desert, is the hottest place in

The Great Plains lie in the midwestern part of the United States.

the United States, with a record high of 134° Fahrenheit (57° Celsius).

East of the Rockies spread the Great Plains. This is the nation's richest food-producing

The Mississippi River in Minneapolis, Minnesota

region. Corn, wheat, and other grains cover the rich soil. Cattle graze on the flat fields.

America's greatest river, the Mississippi, begins in Minnesota. It flows all the way to the Gulf of Mexico.

Early Americans

For millions of years, no people lived in America. Around 18,000 years ago, the Solutrean people came from Europe. Later a second group of hardy hunters from Siberia arrived. These were the ancestors of today's American Indians.

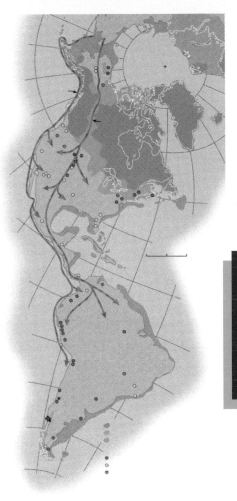

A map showing the migration of the earliest peoples to arrive in North America and South America

For thousands of years, these people lived undisturbed. Then European explorers discovered North America.

A painting showing Spanish conquistador Francisco Vasquez de Coronado exploring what is now New Mexico

In 1492, Italian explorer Christopher Columbus, sailing from Spain, landed in the New World, in the Caribbean islands. Spanish conquistadors ("conquerors") followed. Soon

Great Britain, France, and Holland were establishing settlements in the land that would become the United States, Canada, and Mexico.

In 1607, English colonists founded Jamestown, Virginia, the first permanent English settlement in America.

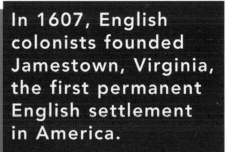

By the early 1700s, there were thirteen colonies. These colonies belonged to Great Britain. This meant that the British government could make rules and collect taxes. In 1775, the Americans rebelled and the

American colonists fought the Revolutionary War to win independence from England.

In 1776, American leaders signed the Declaration of Independence, which proclaimed freedom from British rule.

Revolutionary War began. The British and Americans fought for 8 long years. Finally, Britain recognized the United States as an independent nation.

Moving Forward

The first Europeans came to America for many reasons. Some, like the conquistadors, wanted to get rich. Others came in search of a place to practice their religion in safety. Many were unhappy and wanted to have a new start in a new land.

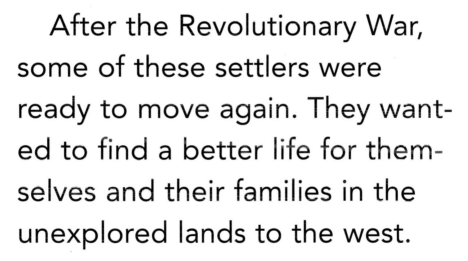

Pioneer families heading to the American West in the early 1800s

After the Revolutionary War, some of these settlers were ready to move again. They wanted to find a better life for themselves and their families in the unexplored lands to the west.

As these pioneers moved west, they fought with the

American Indians. Thousands of American Indians were killed. Even more died of diseases brought from Europe. Others were forced onto reservations.

African Americans also suffered during the early years. Beginning in 1619, thousands of Africans were brought to America as slaves. They were owned by the people they worked for and were not paid for their work. They had no rights as citizens. Often, their owners mistreated them.

African slaves being sold at an auction in the United States in the 1800s

Many people thought slavery was wrong. During the Civil War, northern states that would not allow slavery fought the southern slave states. Finally, in 1865, more than 3 million African Americans were freed from slavery.

In 1929, the Great Depression began. This led to many years of hard economic times. Racial prejudice continued to make life unfair for many people of color. The Civil Rights Movement of the 1950s and 1960s tried to address this problem.

During the Great Depression, hungry people lined up for food at soup kitchens (left). Martin Luther King, Jr., led the Civil Rights Movement, which sought equality for all Americans (right).

In 1969, Americans became the first humans to land on the moon (right). Computers were an important part of American life in the early 2000s (below).

The late 1900s were a time of change and challenge. Technology grew rapidly and the United States and the Soviet Union "raced to the moon." Americans added computers, microwave ovens, and cell phones to their lives.

A Diverse People

America's history is filled with stories of brave people who left their own countries to immigrate, or move forever, to the United States. Like the early settlers, these people wanted a better life. Between 1820 and 1996, millions of immigrants came from all over the world.

American schoolchildren

First came large numbers of immigrants from Germany, Ireland, and Italy. These were followed in the late 1800s and early 1900s by people from Central and Eastern Europe, Russia, China, and Japan. In the late 1900s, people from Southeast Asian and Latin American countries emigrated to the United States.

Today, the United States has an interesting mix of people from all over the world. About 1 in 100 is American Indian. Approximately 72 percent of Americans are of European heritage. The African-American population makes up 13 percent of the 275 million people in the United States. Hispanics make up 11 percent of the

Today, the United States is made up of people of many different ethnic groups.

population, and Asians and Pacific Islanders make up about 4 percent.

When people immigrate to the United States, they bring their religions with them. There are 1,230 religious organizations in the United States! When people are asked what their religious preference is, about 59 percent say Protestant; 25 percent, Catholic; 2 percent, Jewish; 3 percent, Muslim or other; and 7 percent, none.

The Economy

The United States imports, or buys, more than it sells, or exports, to other countries. Machinery, airplanes and other vehicles, chemicals, scientific instruments, and televisions are the major exports. Major American farm products include animal feeds, corn, meat, soybeans, and wheat.

An automobile factory (above) and a soybean field (right)

Copper, gold, lead, silver, titanium, and zinc are among the nation's many natural resources.

The United States has one of the highest standards of living in the world. This means that the average American has more money than the average person from almost any other country.

A high standard of living depends on having citizens who have the skills to earn a good living. Americans believe that all children should get a good education. In most states, children must go to school until they are at least 16 years old.

Over two-thirds of public high schoolers remain in school until they graduate. Each year, more and more Americans go

Harvard University (left) is one of the nation's finest universities. Most people in the United States live in urban areas, such as Washington, D.C. (above).

to college. In the 1990s, more than one million people graduated each year.

American life continues to change. A century ago many Americans lived on farms. Now almost every one lives in an urban area.

A Democratic Government

The U.S. Congress

President George W. Bush

The U.S. Supreme Court

The United States is a democracy. Its people make the decisions about how the country is run. They elect representatives, or legislators, who vote for the laws and make the voice of the people heard.

Washington, D.C., is the nation's capital. The federal government there has three branches. Congress, the legislative branch, creates the laws. The executive branch, headed by the U.S. president, carries out the laws passed by Congress. The judicial branch, headed by the Supreme Court, makes sure that people follow the laws. The division of government into these three branches happens at the state and local levels, too.

A Rich Culture

The United States is often called the Land of Immigrants because most Americans have roots in some other country. When immigrants come to the United States, they add their traditions, celebrations, foods, and languages to American culture.

Irish dancers during a St. Patrick's Day parade in Chicago (left), an American Indian powwow in New Mexico (bottom left), and a Chinese New Year celebration in Boston (bottom right)

Some kinds of music, such as African-American spirituals or gospel songs, can be traced directly to an immigrant group. African Americans were also the first jazz musicians. Now Americans of many

Jazz (left) and country western (above) are two kinds of music that originated in the United States.

different ethnic backgrounds—as well as musicians around the world—create and play jazz.

The United States is also the birthplace of many other kinds of music, including the blues, rock and roll, rap, hip-hop, and country western.

An American eating Japanese food

Many popular "American" foods came from another country. Mexican Americans introduced tacos and burritos. Spaghetti and pizza come from Italy. Many Americans love Chinese egg rolls. Lots of non-Irish people join Irish-Americans eating corned beef and cabbage on St. Patrick's Day.

Some foods that people now eat in other countries began in the United States. Native Americans showed the early settlers how to make popcorn and get syrup from maple trees. Americans became the first people to have cold cereal for breakfast when Dr. John Kellogg invented cornflakes.

Americans play lots of different sports. Some of these sports, such as hockey, soccer,

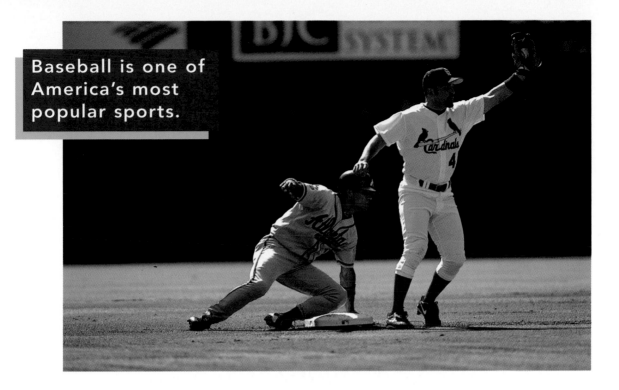

Baseball is one of America's most popular sports.

and rugby, began in other countries. Other sports, such as baseball, basketball, and football, were invented in the United States.

The United States supports many different arts. Every year,

more than 11 million people attend one of the hundreds of Broadway plays in New York City. Most major American cities have a professional ballet company, symphony orchestra, theater, and several museums.

Hollywood, California, is considered the film capital of the world. Thousands of movies are made in the Hollywood area every year!

The United States has a rich culture, many natural resources,

The Statue of Liberty is a powerful symbol for people who have come to the United States in search of a better life.

and great beauty. American people have a very high standard of living. But what makes America unique is the rich blend of people from all over the world.

To Find Out More

Here are some additional resources to help you learn more about the United States of America:

 **Books**

Maestro, Betsy. **The New Americans: Colonial Times, 1620-1689.** Lothrop, Lee & Shepard Books, 1998.

Morley, Jacqueline, and David Antram. **Exploring North America.** Peter Bedrick Books, 1996.

Petersen, David. **North America** (True Books). Children's Press, 1998.

Quiri, Patricia Ryon. **The Declaration of Independence** (True Books). Children's Press, 1998.

Sakurai, Gail. **The Thirteen Colonies** (Cornerstones of Freedom). Children's Press, 2000.

Stevens, Kathryn. **The United States** (Faces and Places). The Child's World, Inc., 2000.

Thompson, Gare. **Immigrants: Coming to America.** Children's Press, 1997.

Wormser, Richard. **American Childhoods.** Walker & Co., 1996.

✦ Organizations and Online Sites

**Ben's Guide to
U.S. Government**
http://bensguide.gpo.gov/

Ben Franklin is your virtual guide to the branches of U.S. government and how they started. Learn about citizenship, elections, symbols, and more. Play a game or two along the way! Separate sections for varying grade levels, parents, and teachers.

CIA World Factbook—USA
*http://www.odci.gov/cia/
publications/factbook/it.html*

Facts on America's people, geography, government, economy, and more, put together by the United States Central Intelligence Agency.

Explore United States
*http://www.eplay.com/
1998-1226/etravel/cow.adp*

Special feature from ePLAY about the famous people, places, and events in colonial America and the Revolutionary War. Includes a glossary of colonial terms.

Intellicast: USA Weather
*htttp://www.intellicast.com/
LocalWeather/World/
UnitedStates/Navigation/*

Forecasts and weather for the USA. Includes radar, satellite images, and maps.

The National Geographic Society
*http://www.
nationalgeographic.com/*

Use the Map Machine to find atlas information, physical and political maps, and satellite images of the United States.

Important Words

diverse varied

erosion slow wearing away of rock or another material by weather and other natural forces

federal relating to a nation formed by the union of several states

heritage background

New World The Western Hemisphere, especially North America and South America

preference choice

prejudice dislike of or unfair treatment of people simply because they are different from oneself

rebelled rose up against the ones in power

reservation piece of land set aside for a certain group of people

unique being the only one of its kind

Index

Meet the Authors

Christine Petersen grew up on the shores of the Pacific Ocean in California, and now lives in the beautiful lake country near Minneapolis, Minnesota. She is a biologist and an educator, and has spent years researching and lecturing about North American bats. Christine likes to hike and snowshoe, read, play with her two cats, and travel.

David Petersen is Christine Petersen's father. He has enjoyed writing True Books for more than twenty years. David lives in Colorado, where he hikes, hunts, fishes, camps, explores, and studies nature.